Cooking Chinese Food at Home

Paul Higham

Contents

Takeaway at home 5
Utensils 5
   Woks 5
      Seasoning your wok 6
   Wok Stand 6
   Food Slicer or Chinese hok 6
   Strainer 7
Methods of Cooking 7
   Stir Fry 7
   Deep Frying 8
   Steaming 8
   Shallow Frying 9
   Boiling 9
General Notes 10
   The MSG phobia 10
   The fermented sauces issue 11
   Reformed Chicken 11
Preparation 13
   Pre Cooked Meats 13
   Pre cooked chicken 13
   Fried Rice Dishes 13
   Spring Rolls 14
Chinese Takeaway Style Cooking 15
Sauces 16
   Sweet and Sour Sauce 16
   Hot and Garlic Sauce 17

Pineapple Sauce 18

Kung Po Sauce 19

Hot Sweet and Spicy Sauce 20

Satay Sauce 21

Lemon Sauce 22

Orange Sauce 23

Cantonese Sauce 24

Sesechuan Sauce 25

OK Sauce 26

Chinese Curry Sauce 28

Soups 30

Chicken and Sweetcorn Soup 30

Crab and Sweetcorn Soup 31

Duck Soup 32

Hot and Sour Soup 33

Won ton soup 34

Chicken and mushroom soup 36

Chicken noodle soup 37

Mixed Vegetable Soup 38

Starters 39

Spare ribs with barbeque sauce 39

Spare ribs with sweet and sour sauce 40

Spare ribs with hot sweet and spicy sauce 41

Salt and pepper spare ribs 42

Prawn Toast 43

Crispy Aromatic Duck 44

Crispy Aromatic Lamb 45

Crispy Seaweed 46

Spring Rolls 47

Duck Rolls 48

Prawn Rolls 49

Vegetable spring rolls 50

Chicken wings in OK sauce 51

Chicken wings in hot and spicy sauce 52

Satay chicken on skewers 53

Pork and Prawn sui mai 54

Deep fried won tons 55

Seafood Dishes 57

King prawns with green peppers and black bean sauce 57

Szechuan king prawns 58

Kung Po king prawns 59

King prawns with bamboo shoots and water chestnuts 60

King prawn chop suey 61

Squid with green peppers and black bean sauce 62

Squid in satay sauce 63

Mussels in satay sauce 64

Beef Dishes 65

Beef Chow Mein 65

Crispy Chilli Beef 66

Beef in Black Bean Sauce 67

Beef in Szechuan Sauce 68

Beef Chop Suey 69

Beef Fried Rice	70
Chicken Dishes	71
Chicken Fried Rice	71
Chicken Chow Mein	72
Chinese Chicken Curry	73
Chicken Chop Suey	74
Sweet and sour chicken	75
Chicken in Yellow bean Sauce with cashews	76
Lemon Chicken	77
Chicken with bamboo shoots and water chestnuts	78
Chicken with pineapple	79
Pork Dishes	80
Chinese Roast Pork	80
Crispy Pork Balls	81
Sweet and Sour Pork	82
Hot, sweet and Spicy Chinese Roast Pork with beansprouts	83
Chinese Roast Pork Chow Mein	84
Pork with Tomatoes	85
Pork with mushrooms	86
Pork with bamboo shoots and water chestnuts	87
Pork with green peppers and black bean sauce	88
Special Dishes	89
Special Foo Yung	89
Special Omelette	90
Singapore Fried Rice	91
Acknowledgements	92

Takeaway at home

If you have ever been to your favorite Chinese takeaway and thought, this is great but I wonder why every time I try to cook it at home it's not the same, this is the book for you.
In the course of my research for this book, I have cooked in many different takeaways just so that I could learn the secrets of the trade. Many of these recipes are not common knowledge, but nearly all of them share a common theme. They MUST be able to be cooked quickly so as to maximize profit for the owners of the restaurant.
This book lists some authentic recipes as found in a lot of Chinese takeaways in the UK. Please experiment using the base recipes as a starting point. If you wish to see a recipe that is not included in the book, please let me know on my website. www.paulhigham.co.uk

Utensils

Utensils used to cook authentic Chinese Takeaway food at home are very simple and easily available. The main utensil is a good wok. This can be used for nearly all your dishes and is very inexpensive. A good knife or Chinese hok is also essential along with a heavy cook's knife or chopper. Although a rice cooker is useful to have, a pan will suffice. You will also need a strainer or sieve and a metal ladle or spatula. Please note that if you have only a non-stick wok, then please do not use metal in it. It will destroy the non-stick coating. Use either a wooden spoon or plastic spatula and ladle.

Woks

A good wok is the heart of the Chinese takeaway. There are many different types of wok, ranging from flat bottomed non-stick (for electric hobs) to the original carbon steel woks found in every Chinese takeaway. Woks are readily available from any Chinese wholesaler and are very inexpensive.

I highly recommend a carbon steel wok. A non-stick wok seems like a good option to start with, but with the high temperatures needed to cook authentic Chinese takeaway food these soon degrade and lose their coating. Once this starts, they are next to useless. A carbon steel wok should last a lifetime and are easily and cheaply available from any Chinese wholesaler or online.

When you first buy your carbon wok, it will be clean and silver looking. You will need to season it first to ensure a non-stick coating is applied.

Seasoning your wok

1. Clean the wok with a small amount of detergent in very hot water. This will remove the protective film that the manufacturers of the wok have coated it in for shipping.
2. With a paper towel coated in a small amount of oil, completely coat the inside of the wok.
3. Heat the wok on a high heat until the wok is smoking and the inside of the wok turns a very dark blue / black
4. Remove from the heat and wipe the inside of the wok with a clean paper towel. The paper towel will acquire a dark amount of burnt oil and carbon. Throw away and coat the inside of the wok once again with a very small amount of clean oil.
5. Repeat steps 3 and 4 until the paper towel used for cleaning comes away without any black on it. This usually takes about three to four times. The wok is now ready to use.
6. After using a wok, always just rinse with hot water while the wok is still very hot, wipe with a paper towel and recoat with a thin layer of oil to prevent rust.

Wok Stand

These are usually made from cast iron and enable you to stand a non-flat bottom wok on a normal gas ring. This helps to prevent spilling of hot sauce and also helps the flame to cover more of the wok bottom.

Food Slicer or Chinese hok

A food slicer or sharp knife is essential for getting nice thin slices of meat or vegetables.

Strainer

A strainer or sieve is needed especially when cooking fried rice or other dishes that need draining.

Methods of Cooking

Stir Fry

Stir frying is the classic Chinese cooking method; quick cook over high heat in a small amount of oil, toss and turn the food when it cooks. In stir frying, the food should always be in motion. Spread it around the pan or up the sides of the wok, and then toss it together again in the centre and repeat. This method allows meats to stay juicy and flavourful, vegetables to come out tender-crisp.

There are variations, of course, but the basic pattern for many Chinese dishes is to pre-heat the pan or wok (a drop of water will sizzle when it's hot enough), add the oil and heat it, stir fry the meat, remove it, stir fry the vegetables, return the meat to the pan, add sauce and seasonings, thicken the sauce and serve. Since stir frying is a last-minute operation, one or two stir fry dishes in one meal is the general rule.

Speed is essential in preparing many Chinese dishes. All ingredients should be on hand before stir frying is begun. Meat and vegetables should be thinly sliced or cut into small cubes. Before the oil is introduced the pan should be heated sufficiently so that the oil is free-flowing, and then the ingredients added, and stirred vigorously and continuously during the entire cooking period. The highest heat obtainable must be used, while constantly stirring, since stir-fry dishes can be ruined in a matter of seconds. Burned spots in the pan should be wiped with a paper towel and the pan re-oiled for further use. This rapid form of cooking leaves comparatively little sauce. Since stir-frying requires only a few minutes, such dishes are usually the last to be prepared; obviously, they are at their best when served immediately from the pan. Recommended cooking times are only approximate. Stir frying preserves colour, texture, and taste as well as nutritional values.

It is good practice to wipe out your wok immediately after use and then it is ready for use again.

Deep Frying

Deep frying is essential to the Chinese takeaway. Certain main dishes also call for meats to be deep fried for a crunchy coating, and then stir fried to combine them with vegetables and flavourings. The oil must be at the right temperature to cook food properly. The most food-proof method is to use a thermostatically controlled electric fryer. If you deep fry in your wok or pot, use a frying thermometer, or test the oil before adding food by dropping in a small piece of meat or vegetable. If it sizzles and skates around the surface of the oil, the temperature is right. If it sinks, the oil is not hot enough. If it browns too quickly, and the oil smokes, the temperature is too high. Oil can be reduced if you strain it and add fresh oil each time. Keep a separate batch for frying fish and seafood.

Deep frying is another common method of Chinese food preparation. For this a deep fryer or a deep saucepan with a wire basket which fits inside it, is most convenient. Chinese cooks use two temperatures of oil for deep frying. In general, when the oil begins to smoke, it is ready to fry pork and beef, the tougher meats. When the oil begins to bubble, which is at a temperature slightly lower, it is suitable for chicken and kidneys. Chinese cooks use vegetable oil and lard. Either peanut or sesame oil, or other prepared vegetable oils are suitable.

Steaming

The Chinese steam their food in woven bamboo trays that stack one atop the other. The beauty of this system is that several foods cook at one time, saving fuel. All sorts of foods are steamed: meats, fish, dumplings, buns stuffed with meat or a sweet bean paste-bread! For best results, the water should be boiling when the food goes into the steamer and the flame should be high enough to keep it boiling.

After a high heat has brought the water to a boil, and the ingredients inserted, the heat is lowered as the steaming process begins (to avoid vibrations and a burned pot). If the food has been placed initially on a serving platter, there will be no need to transfer it to another platter for serving at the table. Once cooked, food should not be left in the steamer unless the heat has been turned off before cooking is complete, after which the cooking process continues for a few minutes. Thus overcooking is avoided.

Steaming preserves flavours and food nutrients through the use of steam temperature rather than higher temperatures that destroy or leach these values in discarded boiling water. Several tiers can be used in the steamer to cook different foods simultaneously. Cooking time usually varies between 15 to 30 minutes for meat patties but can range from 20 minutes to 5 hours (which may require more water), depending upon the type of food to be steamed. However, meats cooked in this fashion must be of top quality. Chinese steamed foods are to be consumed right away - these foods are delicate and cooked to perfection. Reheating leftover steamed meats, steamed fish and seafood often become soggy and limp and lose flavour upon reheating.

Shallow Frying
Shallow frying requires medium heat and a longer cooking time than deep frying. After heating sufficient oil to cover the entire bottom of the pan, ingredients are spread evenly in the pan and allowed to fry slowly for a few minutes, turned over once or twice, browning both sides. This technique seals in juices in meats and is particularly useful for the final cooking of pre-fried or pre-boiled foods.

Boiling
In parboiling, ingredients are cut and washed first, then put in a large pot in which they can float freely, over high heat. Vegetables to be eaten crisp, like broccoli, are removed from the water just before they come to a full boil; those that cannot be eaten raw or take a long time to cook should remain in the pot for whatever time is required after boiling starts. Slow and prolonged boiling destroys flavour to some degree and certainly much nutritional value is lost in the boiling water that is discarded. Parboiled ingredients are poured with the water into a colander, rinsed or soaked in cold water until thoroughly cooled, and used as the recipe

directs, or in salads. Parboiled vegetables are often used in banquet dishes where time may be limited. For full boiling, as in preparing soups, the Chinese employ a slow simmering process. As soon as the water boils, the heat is turned low and the soup allowed to simmer for whatever period of time is necessary. However, preparing soups by rapid boiling in which intense heat is used will result in the same preservation of colour, texture, shape, and nutrition as in tossed cooking.

General Notes

The MSG phobia

Nothing in Chinese cookery causes as much opposite emotion as MSG. There are many sites on the internet dedicated to proving it is bad for you as those that are insistent that it is in no way harmful at all. I don't really have any strong feelings at all on MSG. Like any other food stuff, I believe that as long as it is used as part of range of different foodstuffs, it won't do you much harm. (I'm sure I will get many emails about this!!)

The one thing that is important is that most if not all Chinese takeaways use MSG in many of their recipes. Why?

In order to understand why, it's easier to let you know what MSG does. Many books pronounce MSG as a flavour enhancer and it is. They then usually offer the proviso that if the food is fresh enough, then MSG is not needed. This is slightly misleading.

MSG works by fooling the tongue and therefore the body by introducing a chemical reaction on the tongue which thinks that the food contains far more protein than it actually does. The body is geared to think of protein as a super food and therefore tastes good. (Many chefs have now labelled this UMAMI flavour which is not strictly true). It is used by Chinese takeaways (And also many other food manufacturers) to make the food more tasty and also to fool the body into thinking that the food is far more nutritious than it actually is.

Once the food is eaten, the body, geared up for a large amount of protein which it hasn't received, starts to feel hungry again after a short amount of time. (Does this sound familiar?)

So a Chinese takeaway can put less meat in chicken fried rice, and make it taste filling and nutritious. (At least for a short time) One thing is for sure. If you want to make takeaway food at home that tastes like your local Chinese, you need to get hold of some MSG. (This can be bought easily and cheaply online)

In the USA, you can buy it under the name Accent, which is pure MSG.

The fermented sauces issue

In a cookbook that is designed to allow you how to cook authentic takeaway food at home, it is tempting to get right down to the basic level and give recipes on how to create ALL the sauces used in the Chinese takeaway kitchen. However, in takeaways most of the sauces are bought in, and nothing is truer than for fermented sauces. Sauces of this type which contain fermented beans and grain are difficult to make at home, time consuming and are often widely different to the taste that you would expect in a takeaway. So, to ensure the authentic taste the following sauces should be bought.

Soy, Hoi sin, Yellow bean, black bean, chilli and Oyster sauces.

Many of these can be bought at your local supermarket now, but are also widely available online from Chinese wholesalers. However I have included some recipes for these sauces in the glossary at the end of the book. In essence, if buying in fermented sauces, it is usually better to go for the paste concentrates and add stock to them during the cooking process.

Reformed Chicken

Although all the chicken recipes in this book use pieces of chicken that are easily obtainable, there does seem to be a worrying trend in many takeaways to use reformed chicken in place of the real thing. What is reformed chicken?

Chicken carcasses from which all of the meat has been removed are washed under a high pressure hot hose. This gets all the particles of meat and fat from the chicken and makes them into a soupy emulsion. To this lactose, starch, salt, preservative and stabiliser are added. The mixture is then heated up to boiling point to kill any organisms and then the emulsion is spun at high speeds to remove all the excess water. The remaining sludge is then compressed into blocks of reformed meat. Use this if you would like to get the REAL authentic taste of some cheap takeaways. Myself – I'll stick to real chicken thanks very much.

Preparation

The single most important thing about cooking Chinese takeaway food is to be well prepared before even putting your wok on. Since most of the food is cooked in a very small amount of time, it is essential to have all your preparation done before adding anything to the wok. Things like slicing meat, vegetables and sauces should all be complete before starting. Also it is to your advantage to have next to you in the kitchen things like Oil, stock, salt, sugar, MSG, soy sauce and cornflour mixed with a little water. Keep these in bowls next to your hob for easy access.

Pre Cooked Meats

In the majority of Chinese take away dishes the meat content can be cooked from a raw state. In several dishes the meat needs to be pre-cooked. These are the Chinese roast pork, spare ribs and the chicken and pork used in the sweet and sour dishes. The prawn in the sweet and sour dishes can be battered and cooked from raw.

If cooking any of the sweet and sour dishes for future use, batter the pork, chicken or prawn and cook to half way. Store in plastic containers and deep freeze. When required they can be deep fried in hot oil straight from the freezer.

Pre cooked chicken

You can either purchase pre cooked chicken or cook it yourself. An easy way to cook chicken is to place it in a plastic bowl and just about cover it with water. Cover the bowl with cling film and then place in a microwave for five to ten minutes until cooked. This will cook the chicken without imparting flavour. You can also pre-cook chicken by poaching the chicken in a pan on the hob in the same way.

Fried Rice Dishes

For fried rice dishes the rice needs to be cooked and cooled. Cooking a batch of boiled rice and storing in the fridge or freezer can be a great time saver for the coming week. If storing in the fridge or freezer, the rice should be kept in plastic containers with lids. Using this method the rice keeps very well indeed. The most important part of cooking with rice is that it is dry and cold. This will prevent it sticking to your wok.

Spring Rolls

Spring rolls can be cooked to a half way stage and then stored in the freezer until needed. You can then finish off the spring roll straight from the freezer when cooking.

Chinese Takeaway Style Cooking

Takeaway cooking is different to the more relaxed version of the restaurant style in that all dishes need to be cooked in a short a time as possible. Most of the following dishes should be cooked in less than 3-4 minutes

In essence, it is perfectly acceptable to swap and change meats, vegetables and sauces around to invent your own special dishes. At the end of the main meals there is a selection called special selection. These consist of the specials that are usually found in all Chinese takeaways. You may omit any meat or vegetables that you desire but in general you should stick to having 4oz of meat, 4oz of veg and sauce, in any combination.

In some takeaways fried rice dishes are served with a sauce. Feel free to add any of the sauces to any fried rice dish. The best thing to do is experiment.

In a takeaway meat is usually put into the wok first. Depending on the vegetables needed the meat can be removed or left in the wok whilst the vegetables are cooking. Small sweetcorn and carrots may need a longer cooking time, so remove the meat if you think that it will be overcooked. By practising with your wok, you will quickly get the hang of what you can get away with. But remember; do not overcook your meat. Even pork and chicken do not need a long cooking time as you will have cut the meat up into smaller pieces than other types of cookery.

Sauces

The heart of Chinese takeaway is the sauce that the food is served in. In order to make authentic Chinese takeaway sauces, follow the recipes below and store them in the fridge for use when needed. If you are just cooking a single serving, make the sauce fresh if you like, but having a store of ready-made sauces in the fridge or freezer will cut down your cooking times enormously.

Sweet and Sour Sauce

4 tbsp Tomato Sauce
3 tbsp White vinegar
4 tbsp Sugar
100 ml of Chicken stock
½ Lemon
1 small Onion (Sliced into matchsticks)
1 small Carrot (Sliced into matchsticks)
Cornflour
1 tbsp Vegetable oil
1 slice Pineapple

Heat the oil in a hot wok. Add the onion and carrot and stir for a few seconds. Add the tomato sauce, vinegar, lemon juice, sugar and stock. Heat at maximum until simmering. Add the cornflour mixed with water to thicken sauce. A sliced and chopped pineapple may be added to the sauce according to taste.

Tip: Heat the wok until a splash of water added to it will instantly boil up and turn to steam. This is hot enough. Then add the oil to the hot wok.

Hot and Garlic Sauce

4 tbsp Tomato Sauce
3 tsp Chili powder
3 tsp Garlic Sauce
1 tsp sugar
100 ml Chicken stock
Dash red powder for colouring
Cornflour mixed in water

Heat the wok until slightly smoking. Add the garlic, chilli powder and tomato sauce. Stir well in the wok. Add the stock and the sugar. Simmer for a few minutes to allow the flavours to develop and then add a small amount of cornflour to thicken. Cornflour mixed with water will thicken once the sauce is boiling. Once the required thickness is reached, add some red powder for colouring.

Pineapple Sauce

Half a pineapple pureed
Slice of pineapple chopped
1 tbsp seasoned oil
1 small onion cut into chunks
1 tbsp light soy sauce
1 small green pepper, cut into chunks
1 small carrot, cut into thin julienne strips
2 tbsps soft brown sugar
3 tbsps rice vinegar
100 ml of stock or water
1 tbsp thin cornflour paste

Heat the oil, add the vegetables and stir fry for about 1 minute, then add all the ingredients with the stock or water and bring to the boil. Add the cornflour paste gradually a little at a time to thicken the sauce to the desired consistency. Add the chopped pineapple and stir well and save for use.

Kung Po Sauce

1 tbsp seasoned oil
1 small onion cut into chunks
1 tbsp light soy sauce
1 small green pepper, cut into chunks
1 small carrot, cut into thin julienne strips
2 tbsps soft brown sugar
3 tbsps rice vinegar
1 tbsp tomato puree
1 tps of chili powder (or to taste)
100 ml of stock or water
1 tbsp thin cornflour paste

Heat the oil, add the vegetables and stir fry for about 1 minute, then add all the ingredients with the stock or water and bring to the boil. Add the cornflour paste gradually a little at a time to thicken the sauce to the desired consistency. Stir well and Serve.

Hot Sweet and Spicy Sauce

4 tbsp. Tomato sauce.
3 tsp. Chili Powder.
3 tsp. Garlic Powder.
6 tsp. Sugar.
100ml of Chicken stock (or cube).
Dash of red powder (for colouring).
Cornflour.

Heat oil in wok and add chilli powder, garlic powder, and tomato sauce. Mix in. Add stock then sugar. Simmer for a few minutes and add a dash of yellow powder for colouring. Mix in. If necessary add cornflour mixed with water to thicken sauce.

Satay Sauce

1 tbsp. Chilli powder
1 tbsp. Garlic powder
2 tbsp. Peanut butter
1 tbsp. Curry powder
1 tbsp. Sugar
2 tsp. Mustard
2 tsp. Soy sauce
1 tsp. MSG
75 ml Chicken Stock (or cube)
Cornflour

Heat chicken stock in pan. Mix in all ingredients and simmer for a few minutes until well mixed in. To thicken sauce, add cornflour mixed with a little cold water.

Lemon Sauce

Juice of two lemons
100 gms Sugar
Pinch of salt
100 ml Water
Dash of yellow powder (for colouring)
Cornflour (for thickening)

Mix water, sugar, lemon juice and salt. Bring to the boil and simmer for a few minutes. Add a
dash of yellow powder for colouring. Use cornflour mixed with a little water to thicken sauce.

Orange Sauce

2 Large oranges
100 ml water
1 tsp. Lemon juice
Zest from 1/2 orange
1 tbsp. Sugar
Dash of yellow powder(for colouring)
Cornflour (for thickening)

Cut zest from orange. Squeeze the juice from oranges and pour into pan with water. Bring to
maximum heat. Add lemon juice and zest of orange. Simmer until liquid has reduced to about
half. Add sugar. To thicken sauce add cornflour mixed with a little cold water.

Cantonese Sauce

3 small Spring onions
1/2 tsp. Garlic powder
1/2 tsp. Ginger powder
1 tbsp. Soy sauce
1/2 Sugar
Salt to taste
1 tsp. M.S.G.
100 ml of Chicken stock (or cubes)
Cornflour

Finely chop spring onion. Heat oil in wok, add spring onion and stir fry adding all ingredients.
Simmer for a few minutes and mix in. To thicken sauce add cornflour mixed with a little cold
water.

Sesechuan Sauce

1 pint stock
1 tbsp rice wine
1 tbsp wine or cider vinegar
2 tbsps light soy sauce
1 teaspoon chilli powder
1-2 tbsp cornflour
salt and pepper
1 teaspoon MSG
2 tbsps seasoned oil
1 teaspoon sesame oil
1 teaspoon garlic paste
1 teaspoon ginger paste
1 tbsp tomato puree
1 tbsp brown sugar
1 tbsp Hoi Sin Sauce

Heat the oil in a hot wok. Add all the ingredients except stock and salt and pepper and stir fry until hot. Add the stock and bring to the boil, reduce to a simmer and simmer for 5 minutes then season to taste. Now thicken by adding the cornflour paste a little at a time. Recheck and adjust seasoning if needed.

OK Sauce

8 oz tomato Ketchup.
8 oz sugar
4 oz brown sauce(HP preferably)
1/2 tsp chinese 5 spice powder.

Place all ingredients into a saucepan and bring to a rolling boil. stir for 1 min and then turn heat down low and simmer for 10 minutes making sure sauce does not stick to bottom of pan or burn. It should by now have thickened into a sticky sauce.
Store in a glass Jar and let go cold before putting lid on.
To make a sauce for cooking Take 1 tablespoon of thick sauce and add 1 cup of water and simmer in a pan. In a small dish place 1 tablespoon of corn flour and 2 tablespoons of water and mix well.
Add cornflour mix slowly into sauce while stirring until it starts to thicken.

Chinese Gravy

Shin of Beef or cheap beef cut on bone
2-3 spring onions, each tied in a knot and bruised
3-4 pieces root ginger, unpeeled, bruised
3-4 tbsps chinese spirit or brandy
2 1/2 pints water
1 tsp salt
4 tbsps light soy sauce
3 tbsps dark soy sauce
1 tbsp five spice powder
4oz brown sugar

Cut the beef into 2-3 long strips, place them with the spring onions, ginger , brandy and water in a pot, bring to the boil and skim off the scum; simmer very gently under a lid for 20-25 minutes. Add the salt, soy sauce, spice and sugar and return to the boil, then simmer, covered again for 2 hours. Strain the liquid and refrigerate when cold.

Chinese Curry Sauce

1 Pint veg. Oil
1 Onion (large)
1 Carrot (large)
4 Bay leaves
6 Garlic cloves
4 Star anise
1 tsp. Five spice powder
1 Stick of cinnamon
3oz. Coconut cream
1 tsp. Salt
1 Tbsp. Sugar
1 tsp. Cumin powder
3 tsp. Chilli powder
8oz. Curry powder
1 tsp. Turmeric powder
1lb. Plain flour
Chicken stock (or cubes)
Peel from 1/2 orange

Cut up onion and carrot into small pieces. Heat oil in pan and place on very low heat. Add onion and carrot. Simmer for about thirty minutes before adding bay leaves, orange peel, salt, sugar, cumin powder, garlic moons, star anise, five spice powder and cinnamon. Continue simmering on very low heat (avoid burning) until all ingredients have pulped let pan cool a little before sieving through strainer. Re-heat and add coconut cream. Add chilli powder and turmeric powder.

Slowly add curry powder and continue stirring until all mixed in. Slowly add flour, stirring until ingredients turn into a very stiff paste, almost solid. The curry paste is ready for use or can be stored in fridge or freezer for future use.
Now after that recipe you need to know that most Chinese takeaways would never normally make their curry sauce from scratch. They always use a curry sauce concentrate which is added to the wok at cooking time along with chicken stock to make the sauce. The easiest way is to use the same brand which is now readily available at Tesco's stores under the name Goldfish Brand Chinese Curry Concentrate.

Soups

Chicken and Sweetcorn Soup

Chicken and sweetcorn soup is possibly the most popular Chinese soup available from takeaways. You can usually find this in any takeaway. It is easy and very quick to make.

2 oz cooked chicken breast
500ml chicken stock
2 oz sweetcorn
1 tbsps light soy sauce
1 large beaten egg
2 teaspoons cornflour
1 tbsp water
1tsp Sugar
1tsp MSG
1tsp Sesame Oil

Add the sesame oil to a hot wok.
Shred the chicken and add to wok along with the sweetcorn.
Add the chicken stock to the wok. Add the soy sauce.
Next mix your cornflour and water and add to the soup to thicken (continually stir the soup while adding the cornflour and water, until the soup has thickened).
Add the beaten egg to the stock and stir gently so the egg cooks in strands.
Season with plenty of salt and pepper, MSG and the sugar
Serve into individual bowls immediately

Note: Many takeaways omit the egg altogether. It is up to you which you prefer

Crab and Sweetcorn Soup

Crab and sweetcorn soup is made in exactly the same way as chicken and sweetcorn soup. You can usually find this in any takeaway. It is easy and very quick to make.

2 oz of canned crab meat
700ml fish stock
2 oz of sweetcorn
1 tbsp light soy sauce
1 large beaten egg
2 teaspoons cornflour
2 tbsps water
1tsp Sugar
1tsp MSG
1tsp Sesame oil

Add the sesame oil to a hot wok.
Shred the crab and add to wok along with the sweetcorn.
Add the fish stock to the wok. Add the Soy sauce.
Next mix your cornflour and water and add to the soup to thicken (continually stir the soup while adding the cornflour and water, until the soup has thickened).
Add the beaten egg to the stock and stir gently so the egg cooks in strands.
Season with plenty of salt and pepper, MSG and the sugar
Serve into individual a bowl immediately
Note: Many takeaways omit the egg altogether. It is up to you which you prefer

Duck Soup

2 oz Shredded duck
2 small slices root ginger
2 oz Button mushrooms sliced
2 spring onions chopped
Salt and Pepper
2 tbps sesame oil
4 leaves Pak Choi coarsely chopped
100 ml chicken or duck stock
1 tsp MSG

Add the oil to a hot wok. Throw in the sliced ginger. Stir fry for about a minute. Add the duck and the mushrooms. Add the pak choi and then the stock. Add the stock. Bring to a simmer and then add the MSG, salt and pepper. Serve immediately.

Hot and Sour Soup

- 100 ml **chicken stock**
- **1 tsp soy sauce**
- **2 oz cup cooked shredded chicken or pork**
- **2 button mushrooms, diced**
- **1 tsp garlic chili sauce**
- **1/4 tsp ground white pepper**
- **2 tsp white vinegar**
- **1 oz canned bamboo shoots, sliced**
- **1 oz tofu, cut into 1/4 inch dice**
- **1/2 tbs cornflour and 1/2 tbs cold water**
- **1 egg, beaten**
- **1 green onion stalks, diced (including tops)**
- **1/2 teaspoon toasted sesame oil**

Add the stock to a hot wok. Add soy sauce, meat, mushrooms, garlic paste.
Add pepper, vinegar, bamboo shoots and tofu
Simmer for two minutes
Bring to boil and add the cornflour mixed with water to thicken slightly
Add the beaten egg slowly into the soup, stirring whilst adding.
Add onions and sesame to soup stir and serve

Won ton soup

2 oz minced pork
2 spring onions, cut into tiny rounds
2 oz canned bamboo shoots, finely chopped
1 egg yolk
15 wonton wrappers, each about 7.5cm square
1 egg white, lightly beaten
salt
2 leaves Cos lettuce or Chinese celery cabbage shredded crosswise into 2.5cm pieces
100 ml chicken stock
2 tsp groundnut or corn oil

For the marinade:
1 tsp salt
½ tsp sugar
1 tsp tin soy sauce
1 tsp thick soy sauce
Black pepper
1 tsp rice wine or sherry
1 tsp cornflour
1 tbsp water
1 tsp sesame oil

Chop the pork by hand or mince it. Put into a large bowl. Pat dry the shrimps. Cut into the size of petits pois and add to the pork. Prepare the marinade: add the salt, sugar, soy sauces, pepper, wine or sherry and potato flour to the pork. Stir in the water in the same direction, 1 tbsp at a time.

Pick up the pork mixture with one or both hands and throw it back into the bowl or on to a flat surface. Repeat this action about 100 times to achieve the desired light and yet firm texture. Add half the spring onion and all the bamboo shoots to the pork mixture, mix well and leave to marinate for 20-30 minutes. Then blend in the sesame oil.

Just before ready to wrap the wontons, stir in the egg yolk which will bind the filling to the wrappers. Wrap the wontons. Bring a large saucepan of salted water to the boil. Blanch the lettuce or cabbage for about 1 minute, remove with a hand strainer or perforated spoon and transfer to bowl. Put the stock in another saucepan and bring to simmering point. Bring the water in the large saucepan to the boil again. Plunge in the wontons, and return to the boil, stirring gently to separate them. Continue to boil, uncovered, for about 3 minutes until the wontons are cooked and float to the surface. Remove with a hand strainer to individual serving bowls. Add the spring onion, oil and the stock.

Chicken and mushroom soup

100g	Chicken (Cooked)
100g	Button Mushrooms
3	Egg Whites (Beaten)
½tbs	Cornflour
700 ml	Chicken Stock
1tsp	MSG
1tbs	Sesame Oil
3	Fresh coriander leaves to garnish

Add the oil to a hot wok. Add the chicken and the mushrooms. Add the stock into the wok. Wait for the stock to boil and then add the cornflour to thicken. Once thickened add the egg whites slowly stirring all the time. Add the salt and MSG.

Garnish with coriander leaves and serve.

Chicken noodle soup

2 oz cooked and sliced chicken
4 oz Thick rice noodles
2 slices ginger
1 tsp soy sauce
100 ml chicken stock
1 tsp MSG
1 tsp Sesame Oil
salt and pepper

Add the noodles to a pan of hot water to separate. Add the oil to a hot wok. Add the ginger and sliced chicken. Add the stock and the soy sauce to the wok. Add the MSG and salt and pepper. Finally add the separated noodles to the soup and stir to a simmer. Serve immediately.

Mixed Vegetable Soup

1 oz Button Mushrooms (Sliced)
1 oz Bamboo shoots
1 oz Sliced carrots
1 oz Baby corn cobs
1 oz Pak Choi
2 oz bean curd
150 ml chicken stock
1 tsp light soy sauce
1 tsp MSG
1 tsp sesame oil

Slice all the vegetables as you like. Heat the oil in a hot wok and add all the vegetables and the bean curd. Heat to a simmer for about five minutes or until the vegetables are cooked but not soggy. Stir in the MSG and soy sauce and add salt and pepper to taste.

Starters

Spare ribs with barbeque sauce

1lb Pork Spare Ribs
2 Tbsp. Golden syrup

2 Tbsp. Hoi Sin Sauce
2 Tbsp. Yellow Bean Sauce
1 Tbsp. Soy Sauce
1 tsp. M.S.G.
Dash of red powder (for colour)

Chop the ribs into small pieces of about a few inches. Mix all the marinade ingredients and add some of the food colouring. Marinade the ribs overnight in the fridge.

Place the ribs on an oven tray and cook for about half an hour on 200 degrees. Shake the tray every now and then to ensure they are cooked on all sides. Drizzle the syrup over the ribs and then cook until they are a reddish brown. Mix the juice from the ribs with the remaining marinade and simmer for a few minutes. Pour sauce over the ribs and serve. You may cook the ribs in advance and then stir fry them for a few minutes and then pour the hot sauce over them to serve.

Spare ribs with sweet and sour sauce

1lb Pork Spare Ribs
2 Tbsp. Golden syrup

4 Tbsp of sweet and sour sauce
1 Tbsp. Soy Sauce
1 tsp. M.S.G.
Dash of red powder (for colour)

Chop the ribs into small pieces of about a few inches. Mix all the marinade ingredients and add some of the food colouring. Marinade the ribs overnight in the fridge.

Place the ribs on an oven tray and cook for about half an hour on 200 degrees. Shake the tray every now and then to ensure they are cooked on all sides. Drizzle the syrup over the ribs and then cook until they are a reddish brown. Mix the juice from the ribs with the remaining marinade and simmer for a few minutes. Pour sauce over the ribs and serve. You may cook the ribs in advance and then stir fry them for a few minutes and then pour the hot sauce over them to serve. You may add some chopped sliced pineapple to the sauce if desired.

Spare ribs with hot sweet and spicy sauce

1lb Pork Spare Ribs
2 Tbsp. Golden syrup

4 Tbsp Hot sweet and spicy sauce
1 tbsp soy sauce
1 tsp. M.S.G.
Dash of red powder (for colour)

Chop the ribs into small pieces of about a few inches. Mix all the marinade ingredients and add some of the food colouring. Marinade the ribs overnight in the fridge.

Place the ribs on an oven tray and cook for about half an hour on 200 degrees. Shake the tray every now and then to ensure they are cooked on all sides. Drizzle the syrup over the ribs and then cook until they are a reddish brown. Mix the juice from the ribs with the remaining marinade and simmer for a few minutes. Pour sauce over the ribs and serve. You may cook the ribs in advance and then stir fry them for a few minutes and then pour the hot sauce over them to serve.

Salt and pepper spare ribs

1 lb spare ribs
1 tsp course salt
1 tsp Szechuan peppercorns
1 tsp black pepper
Pinch of five spice powder
2 tbsp Cornflour
1 red chilli (sliced)
1 spring onion (sliced)

To make the salt and pepper seasoning

Heat the peppercorns in a dry wok for about a minute. Cool and grind to a dust in a pestle or pepper grinder. Mix the salt, black pepper and peppercorn dust together. Mix in the five spice powder and the cornflour.

Fully coat the spareribs in the salt and pepper mix. Marinade overnight in a sealed container in the fridge overnight.

Deep fry the spare ribs in hot oil in a wok or deep fat fryer until they are brown. Usually this takes about five minutes. In a hot wok add a splash of oil and then stir fry the chilli and spring onion for about 30 seconds. Add the spare ribs and sprinkle some of the salt and pepper mixture over the ribs. Mix together and serve immediately.

Prawn Toast

6 slices of white bread
1 oz of raw prawns
1 egg white
1 cup of vegetable oil
¼ cup of sesame seeds
½ teaspoon of cornflour
¼ teaspoon of sesame oil
Salt and pepper

Puree the prawns, egg white, sesame oil and cornflour until smooth, season well.
Spread the mixture on the slices of white bread and Cut off the crusts.
Press the side with prawn mixture into sesame seeds to coat.
Heat up the oil and deep fry for about 3 minutes on each sides until golden brown.
Serve hot.

Crispy Aromatic Duck

1 2kg duckling
2 teaspoon salt
2 teaspoon 5 spice powder

Wash and thoroughly dry the duck. Rub the salt and 5 spice into the duck inside and out and leave for 24-48 hours in a cool dry place. Roast the duck in a hot oven at 180 degrees for 1 hour and 20 minutes. Baste 2-3 times with its own fat. Remove the duck and allow to rest for 10 minutes. Heat the Duck oil in a cast iron frying pan until just beginning to smoke. Cut the duck in half and fry one piece at a time in the frying pan until very crisp on each side. Shred the skin and meat using a pair of forks and serve on a warmed platter. Serve with slices of cucumber and shredded spring onion, hoi sin sauce or plum sauce and thin Chinese pancakes. The pancakes can be bought from an Asian supermarket. The pancakes should either be steamed or cooked in cling film in the microwave for a minute.

Crispy Aromatic Lamb

1 Whole Shoulder Lamb
2 teaspoon salt
2 teaspoon 5 spice powder

Wash and thoroughly dry the Lamb. Rub the salt and 5 spice into the Lamb skin and push as far into the flesh as you can making a few cuts here and there. Leave for 24-48 hours in a cool dry place. Roast the Lamb in a hot oven at 180 degrees for 1 hour and 40 minutes. Baste 2-3 times with its own fat. Remove the Lamb and allow to rest for 20 minutes. Heat the Lamb oil in a cast iron frying pan until just beginning to smoke. Cut the Lamb meat off the bone into 3-4 large pieces. Fry 1-2 pieces at a time in the frying pan until very crisp on each side. Shred the skin and meat using a pair of forks and serve on a warmed platter. You can serve with pancakes and the usual accompaniments for crispy duck but the lamb can also take stronger flavours and will stand chilli sauce or chilli vinegar as an alternative accompaniment.

Crispy Seaweed

450 g (1 lb) spring greens
vegetable oil, for deep frying
2.5 ml (1/2 tsp) salt
5 ml (1 tsp) caster sugar
15 ml (1 tbsp) ground fried fish, to garnish (optional)

Cut off the hard stalks in the centre of each spring green leaf. Pile the leaves on top of each other, and roll into a tight sausage shape. Thinly cut the leaves into fine shreds. Spread them out to dry.

Heat the oil in a wok until hot. Deep fry the shredded greens in batches, stirring to separate them.

Remove the greens with a slotted spoon as soon as they are crispy, but before they turn brown. Drain.

Sprinkle the salt and sugar evenly all over the "seaweed", mix well, garnish with ground fish, if liked, and serve.

Spring Rolls

Spring Roll Skins.
4oz. Beansprouts.
1oz. Small Prawns.
1oz. Chinese Roast Pork.
1 Small Onion.
Veg. Oil (For Deep Frying).
Flour and water paste for sealing.

SEASONINGS
Salt to taste.
1/2 tsp. Sugar.
1/2 tsp. M.S.G.
1 tsp. Soy Sauce.

Wash and drain the beansprouts and prawns. Slice the pork and onions into small pieces. Add the oil to a hot wok. Add the onion, stir fry for 30 seconds. Add the prawns, pork and beansprouts. Quickly stir fray for about 30 seconds. Remove from wok and drain. Leave until cold.
Layout the spring roll pancakes and place about 2oz of the mixture on the nearest end to you. Fold over and fold in the sides so that all the mixture is covered. Brush on flour paste to seal the roll. Deep fry until golden brown or deep fry until half way cooked and then place in plastic container in the fridge or freezer for use later on. They can be deep fried straight from the freezer.

Duck Rolls

Spring Roll Skins
4oz. Beansprouts
2oz cooked duck meat
1 Small Onion
Veg. Oil (For Deep Frying)
Flour and water paste for sealing

Seasoning
Salt to taste
1/2 tsp. Sugar
1/2 tsp. M.S.G
1 tsp. Soy Sauce

Wash and drain the beansprouts. Slice the duck and onions into small pieces. Add the oil to a hot wok. Add the onion, stir fry for 30 seconds. Add the duck and beansprouts. Quickly stir fray for about 30 seconds. Remove from wok and drain. Leave until cold.
Layout the spring roll pancakes and place about 2oz of the mixture on the nearest end to you. Fold over and fold in the sides so that all the mixture is covered. Brush on flour paste to seal the roll. Deep fry until golden brown or deep fry until half way cooked and then place in plastic container in the fridge or freezer for use later on. They can be deep fried straight from the freezer.

Prawn Rolls

Spring Roll Skins
4oz. Beansprouts
2ox small prawns
1 Small Onion
Veg. Oil (For Deep Frying)
Flour and water paste for sealing

SEASONINGS
Salt to taste
1/2 tsp. Sugar
1/2 tsp. M.S.G.
1 tsp. Soy Sauce

Wash and drain the beansprouts and prawns. Slice the onions into small pieces. Add the oil to a hot wok. Add the onion, stir fry for 30 seconds. Add the prawns, and beansprouts. Quickly stir fray for about 30 seconds. Remove from wok and drain. Leave until cold.
Layout the spring roll pancakes and place about 2oz of the mixture on the nearest end to you. Fold over and fold in the sides so that all the mixture is covered. Brush on flour paste to seal the roll. Deep fry until golden brown or deep fry until half way cooked and then place in plastic container in the fridge or freezer for use later on. They can be deep fried straight from the freezer.

Vegetable spring rolls

Spring Roll Skins
4oz. Beansprouts
1oz. mushrooms
1oz. peppers
1 Small Onion
Veg. Oil (For Deep Frying)
Flour and water paste for sealing

Seasoning
Salt to taste
1/2 tsp. Sugar
1/2 tsp. M.S.G.
1 tsp. Soy Sauce

Wash and drain the beansprouts and mushrooms. Slice the peppers and onions into small pieces. Add the oil to a hot wok. Add the onion, stir fry for 30 seconds. Add the mushrooms, peppers and beansprouts. Quickly stir fray for about 30 seconds. Remove from wok and drain. Leave until cold.
Layout the spring roll pancakes and place about 2oz of the mixture on the nearest end to you. Fold over and fold in the sides so that all the mixture is covered. Brush on flour paste to seal the roll. Deep fry until golden brown or deep fry until half way cooked and then place in plastic container in the fridge or freezer for use later on. They can be deep fried straight from the freezer.

Chicken wings in OK sauce

4 chicken wings
1 oz Onions (Chopped)
1 tsp MSG
Salt and pepper to taste
2 fl oz ok sauce

Remove the wing tips from the wings. Cut the wings in half at the joints leaving 8 pieces of wings. Deep fry the wings until golden brown. (Usually about 5-6 minutes). Remove the wings.

In a hot wok add the oil and the onions. Stir fry for about 30 seconds and then add the wings to the wok. Add the sauce and stir fry for another 30 seconds until all the wings are coated with the sauce. Add MSG, salt and pepper to taste. Serve immediately

Chicken wings in hot and spicy sauce

4 chicken wings
1 oz Onions (Chopped)
1 tsp MSG
Salt and pepper to taste
2 fl oz hot and spicy sauce

Remove the wing tips from the wings. Cut the wings in half at the joints leaving 8 pieces of wings. Deep fry the wings until golden brown. (Usually about 5-6 minutes). Remove the wings.

In a hot wok add the oil and the onions. Stir fry for about 30 seconds and then add the wings to the wok. Add the sauce and stir fry for another 30 seconds until all the wings are coated with the sauce. Add MSG, salt and pepper to taste. Serve immediately

Satay chicken on skewers

4 oz Chicken cut into cubes
2 tsp Soy Sauce
1 tsp MSG
Salt and pepper to taste
1 tsp Sesame oil
2 tbsp Satay Sauce

Cut the chicken into 1 inch pieces. Heat the oil in the wok. Stir fry the chicken with the soy sauce, MSG and salt and pepper. Once the chicken is cooked remove and put to one side.

Heat the same wok, add the satay sauce on a medium heat. Meanwhile place the chicken cubes onto the skewers. Once this is done, pour over the hot satay sauce and serve.

Alternatively

Marinade the chicken in the soy sauce, MSG and oil. Add salt and pepper. Leave in fridge for a few hours. Skewer the chicken cubes on the skewers and place on a hot griddle. Keep turning the skewers until chicken has cooked. Heat the satay sauce in a wok until hot. Pour over the chicken and serve.

TIP: To prevent the skewers burning if you cook them on a griddle, soak them for an hour in water before using.

Pork and Prawn sui mai

3 dried Chinese black or Shiitake mushrooms
6 ounces peeled deveined large shrimp
1 green onion
1 teaspoon minced ginger
3/4 cup ground pork
1 tbsp oyster sauce
1 teaspoon Chinese rice wine or dry sherry
1 teaspoon sesame oil
1/2 teaspoon granulated sugar
about 20 gyoza wrappers (or won ton wrappers cut into circles).

Soften the mushrooms by soaking in hot water for 20 to 30 minutes. Squeeze out any excess water. Cut off the stems.

Soak the shrimp in warm, lightly salted water for 5 minutes. Pat dry. Mince the mushrooms, shrimp, and green onion. Combine with the ginger and pork. Stir in the seasonings. Mix the filling ingredients thoroughly.

Lay a gyoza wrapper in front of you. Wet the edges. Put 2 to 3 teaspoons of filling in the middle, taking care not to get too close to the edges. Gather up the edges of the wrapper and gently pleat so that it forms a basket shape, with the top of the filling exposed.

Steam over boiling water until the filling is cooked through (5 to 10 minutes).

Deep fried won tons

Yields about 48 wontons

4 dried black mushrooms
1 leaf bok choy
1 green onion
1 slice ginger
1/2 pound ground pork
1 tbsp dark soy sauce
1 teaspoon sesame oil
1 teaspoon granulated sugar
Pinch of salt
1 egg, lightly beaten
3 cups oil for deep-frying, or as needed
48 wonton wrappers, or as needed
Water, as needed

Wipe any dirt off the mushrooms. Soak in warm water until softened (20 to 30 minutes). Squeeze out the excess water and chop. Wash and shred the bok choy leaf. Wash and dice the green onion. Mince the ginger until you have 1/2 teaspoon.

In a medium bowl, combine the ground pork with the dark soy sauce, sesame oil, sugar and salt. Add the lightly beaten egg and the vegetables. This is the wonton filling.

Heat the oil to 375 degrees Fahrenheit. While the oil is heating, prepare the wontons. Lay a wonton wrapper in front of you. Place a teaspoon of the filling in the middle. Fold up the wonton so that it resembles a nurse's cap, wetting the edges to seal (if you haven't made wontons before, see photo instructions on filling wontons).

Add the won tons to the hot oil, a few at a time, sliding them in carefully. Deep-fry the wontons in batches until they are golden brown, turning to make sure they brown evenly. Drain on paper towels or a tempura rack if you have one. As with egg rolls, wontons should be served as soon as possible, to ensure they remain crispy. Serve with Sweet and Sour Sauce or red rice wine vinegar.

TIP: The wontons can be prepared ahead of time up to the cooking stage and refrigerated or frozen. Bring the wontons back to room temperature before deep-frying.

Seafood Dishes

King prawns with green peppers and black bean sauce

4oz. King Prawns
2oz. Green Peppers
1 Small Onion
2 Tbsp. Veg. Oil
Salt to Taste
1/2 tsp. Sugar
1/2 tsp. M.S.G.
2 tsp. Soy Sauce
3 fl/oz. Chicken Stock (or cube)
Cornflour

Shell prawns and slice down back to remove veins. Thoroughly rinse. Thinly slice onion and cut green peppers into squares. Heat oil in wok. Add onion and stir fry. Add peppers and continue stir fry adding prawns. Add stock, salt, sugar, M.S.G., and soy sauce. Stir fry adding black bean sauce and mix in well. If necessary add cornflour mixed with cold water to thicken sauce. Serve on plate or bowl with rice or chips.

Szechuan king prawns

1Kg (2Lbs) King Prawn
400ml Szechuan sauce
4 tbsps seasoned oil
2 inches root ginger crushed and chopped finely
6 cloves garlic thickly sliced
1 small onion chopped in large chunks
1 tbsp dark soy sauce
Salt and pepper to taste

Peel and de-vein the King Prawn. Heat the oil in a wok until hot and add the onion and cook for 1-2 minutes until translucent but not browning at all. Add the ginger and garlic for a further minute stirring constantly. Now add the King Prawn and seal on all sides. Pour over the Szechuan sauce and simmer until the King Prawn is cooked through.

Kung Po king prawns

king prawns, (in our video are already cooked) 300g
peanuts, half a teacup
5 full dried chillies
2 spring onions
2 cloves of garlic
ginger
2 tbsps of soy sauce
1 teaspoon of sugar
a fresh chilli and a little coriander for garnish

cut the prawns 3/4 along so they "fan"
cut and get ready the above ingredients
heat up the pan, very hot, add 3 tbsps of oil
put the spicy ingredients in the pan, fry until you get a nice aroma
now add the rest of the vegetables, stir
because we used pre-cooked prawns we added them at this point, if raw they go in first.
a minute later add a splash of sesame oil, stir

King prawns with bamboo shoots and water chestnuts

4oz. King Prawns
2oz. Water Chestnuts
1oz. Bamboo Shoots
1 Small Onion
2 Tbsp. Veg. Oil
Salt to Taste
1/2 tsp. Sugar
1/2 tsp. M.S.G.
2 tsp. Soy Sauce
3 fl/oz. Chicken Stock (or cube)
Cornflour

Shell prawns and slice down back to remove veins. Thoroughly rinse. Thinly slice onion and bamboo shoots. Cut water chestnuts into three pieces. Heat oil in wok. Add onion and stir fry. Add water chestnuts and bamboo shoots. Continue stir fry adding prawns. Add stock, salt, sugar, M.S.G., and soy sauce. Stir fry and if necessary add cornflour mixed with water to thicken sauce. Serve on plate or bowl with rice or chips.

King prawn chop suey

4oz. King Prawns
1oz. Water Chestnuts
1oz. Bamboo Shoots
1oz. Mushrooms (Button)
1oz. Carrot (Matchstick Size)
2oz. Beanshoots
1 Small Onion
Salt to taste
1/2 tsp. Sugar
1/2 tsp. M.S.G.
2 tsp. Soy Sauce
3 fl/oz. Chicken Stock (or Cube)
Cornflour

Shell prawns and slice down back to remove veins. Thoroughly rinse. Thinly slice onion. Cut carrot into matchstick size. Cut mushrooms into halves or quarters depending on size. Cut water chestnuts into three pieces and thinly slice bamboo shoots. Wash and drain beanshoots. Heat oil in wok, add onion and stir fry adding carrot, water chestnut and bamboo shoots. Continue to stir fry adding mushrooms then prawns. Quickly stir fry and add bean shoots. Add stock, salt, sugar, M.S.G. and soy sauce. Stir fry and if necessary add cornflour mixed with a little water to thicken sauce. Serve on plate or bowl.

Squid with green peppers and black bean sauce

4oz. Squid
2oz. Green Peppers
1 Small Onion
2 Tbsp. Veg. Oil
Salt to Taste
1/2 tsp. Sugar
1/2 tsp. M.S.G.
2 tsp. Soy Sauce
3 fl/oz. Chicken Stock (or cube)
Cornflour

Shell prawns and slice down back to remove veins. Thoroughly rinse. Thinly slice onion and cut green peppers into squares. Heat oil in wok. Add onion and stir fry. Add peppers and continue stir fry adding prawns. Add stock, salt, sugar, M.S.G., and soy sauce. Stir fry adding black bean sauce and mix in well. If necessary add cornflour mixed with cold water to thicken sauce. Serve on plate or bowl with rice or chips.

Squid in satay sauce

4oz. Squid
1 Small Onion
1 Tbsp. Garden Peas
1 Tbsp. Veg. Oil
2 Tbsp. Satay Sauce (See Sauces)
3 fl/oz. Chicken Stock (or cube)
Cornflour

Rinse squid and cut into strips. You may leave the legs in if they are small, otherwise cut these as well. Thinly slice onion. Make up satay sauce (see sauces). Heat Oil in Wok. Add onion and stir fry, adding squid and peas. Continue stir fry and add stock, Add 2Tbsp. of Satay sauce and mix in. If necessary add cornflour mixed with water to thicken sauce. Serve on plate or bowl with rice or chips.

Mussels in satay sauce

4oz. fresh mussels removed from shells
1 Small Onion
1 Tbsp. Garden Peas
1 Tbsp. Veg. Oil
SEASONING / SAUCE
2 Tbsp. Satay Sauce (See Sauces)
3 fl/oz. Chicken Stock
Cornflour

Rinse mussels. Thinly slice onion. Make up satay sauce (see sauces). Heat Oil in Wok. Add onion and stir fry, adding mussels and peas. Continue stir fry and add stock, Add 2Tbsp. of Satay sauce and mix in. If necessary add cornflour mixed with water to thicken sauce. Serve on plate or bowl with rice or chips.

Beef Dishes

Beef Chow Mein

4oz. Beef topside
4oz. Fine Noodles
1oz. Mushrooms (button)
1oz. Bamboo Shoots
2oz. Beanshoots
1 Small Onion
3 Tbsp. Veg. Oil
Salt to taste
1/2 tsp. Sugar
1/2 tsp. M. S.G.
2 tsp. Soy Sauce
3 fl/oz. Chicken Stock (or Cube)
Cornflour

Put noodles in half pot of boiling water. Stir to loosen strands and drain. Wash and drain beanshoots. Thinly slice beef, onion and bamboo shoots. Cut mushrooms across into four or five pieces. Heat 1 Tbsp. of veg. oil. in wok, Add noodles and stir fry, tossing to avoid sticking. Add beanshoots and mix in well. Put at one side. Heat 2 Tbsp. of oil in wok. Add onion and stir fry, adding chicken. continue stir fry adding bamboo shoots and mushrooms. Add stock, salt, sugar, M.S.G., and soy sauce. Stir fry, and add cornflour mixed with a little water to thicken sauce. Serve noodles on plate or bowl and cover with ingredients. Alternatively mix together and serve.

Crispy Chilli Beef

1/2 teaspoon salt
4 oz. corn starch
1 lb. topside of beef, cut into matchstick strips
2 cups vegetable oil
3 medium carrots, scraped and cut into matchstick strips
2 spring onions, cut into 1 inch sections

Mix the salt and the corn flour together
Mix the strips of beef in the corn flour until fully coated and get rid of excess flour. Deep fry the beef until crispy. (This should take about five minutes). Add the carrots to the fryer when there is about a minute to go. Remove the excess oil from the wok, or take the beef and Carrots out of the deep fat fryer.
Add the Sweet and spicy sauce to the wok and heat until bubbling. Toss the beef and carrots in the sauce. Serve.

Beef in Black Bean Sauce

1Kg (2Lbs) lean Beef
400ml Black Bean sauce
4 tbsps seasoned oil
2 inches root ginger crushed and chopped finely
6 cloves garlic thickly sliced
1 small onion chopped in large chunks
1 tbsp dark soy sauce
Salt and pepper to taste

Cut the Beef into small bite size pieces. Heat the oil in a wok until hot and add the onion and cook for 1-2 minutes until translucent but not browning at all. Add the ginger and garlic for a further minute stirring constantly. Now add the Beef and seal on all sides. Pour over the Black Bean sauce and simmer until the Beef is cooked through.

Beef in Szechuan Sauce

1Kg (2Lbs) lean Beef
400ml Szechuan sauce
4 tbsps seasoned oil
2 inches root ginger crushed and chopped finely
6 cloves garlic thickly sliced
1 small onion chopped in large chunks
1 tbsp dark soy sauce
Salt and pepper to taste

Cut the Beef into small bite size pieces. Heat the oil in a wok until hot and add the onion and cook for 1-2 minutes until translucent but not browning at all. Add the ginger and garlic for a further minute stirring constantly. Now add the Beef and seal on all sides. Pour over the Szechuan sauce and simmer until the Beef is cooked through.

Beef Chop Suey

4oz. Beef (Silverside or Topside)
1oz. Water Chestnuts
1oz. Bamboo Shoots
1oz. Mushrooms
1oz. Carrot (Matchstick Size)
2oz. Beanshoots
1 Small Onion
2 Tbsp. Veg. Oil
Salt to taste
1/2 tsp. Sugar
1/2 tsp. M.S.G.
2 tsp. Soy Sauce
3 fl/oz. Chicken Stock. (or cube)
Cornflour

Thinly slice beef across grain. Thinly slice onion and bamboo shoots. Cut water chestnuts into halves. Cut mushrooms into halves or quarters depending on size. Cut carrot into matchstick size and wash and drain beanshoots. Heat oil in wok, add onion and stir fry. Add beef, carrot and water chestnut. Stir fry adding mushrooms and bamboo shoots. Add beanshoots and stir fry adding stock, salt, sugar, M.S.G., soy sauce. Stir fry and if necessary add cornflour mixed with a little water to thicken sauce. Serve on plate or bowl.

Beef Fried Rice

4oz. Beef (Pre-Cooked)
6oz. Rice (Cooked and Cooled)
1oz. Mushrooms (Button)
1 Egg
1 Small Onion
1 Tbsp. Garden Peas
2 Tbsp. Veg. Oil
Salt to taste
1/2 tsp. Sugar
1/2 tsp. M.S.G.
3 tsp Soy Sauce

Boil rice and cool. Cut beef into small strips. Cut mushrooms into small pieces and onion into small squares. Beat egg in bowl. Heat oil in wok. Add onion and stir fry, adding mushrooms.

Continue stir fry adding beef and peas. Add rice and stir fry or toss to mix in well. Make well in centre and add egg mixture. Stir, scramble and mix in thoroughly. Add salt, sugar, M.S.G., and soy sauce. Stir fry and serve on plate or bowl.

Chicken Dishes

Chicken Fried Rice

4oz. Chicken (Pre-Cooked)
6oz. Rice (Cooked and Cooled)
1oz. Mushrooms (Button)
1 Egg.
1 Small Onion.
1 tbsp. Garden Peas
2 tbsp. Veg. Oil.
Salt to taste.
1/2 tsp. Sugar.
1/2 tsp. M.S.G.
3 tsp Soy Sauce.

Boil rice and cool. Cut chicken into small squares. Cut mushrooms into small pieces and onion into small squares. Beat egg in bowl. Heat oil in wok. Add onion and stir fry, adding mushrooms.
Continue stir fry adding chicken and peas. Add rice and stir fry or toss to mix in well. Make well in centre and add egg mixture. Stir, scramble and mix in thoroughly. Add salt, sugar, M.S.G., and soy sauce. Stir fry and serve on plate or bowl.

Chicken Chow Mein

4oz. Chicken (Breast)
4oz. Fine Noodles
1oz. Mushrooms (button)
1oz. Bamboo Shoots
2oz. Beanshoots
1 Small Onion
3 tbsp. Veg. Oil
Salt to taste
1/2 tsp. Sugar
1/2 tsp. M. S.G.
2 tsp. Soy Sauce
3 fl/oz. Chicken Stock (or Cube)
Cornflour

Put noodles in half pot of boiling water. Stir to loosen strands and drain. Wash and drain beanshoots. Thinly slice chicken, onion and bamboo shoots. Cut mushrooms across into four or five pieces. Heat 1 Tbsp. of veg. oil. in wok, Add noodles and stir fry, tossing to avoid sticking. Add beanshoots and mix in well. Put at one side. Heat 2 Tbsp. of oil in wok. Add onion and stir fry, adding chicken. continue stir fry adding bamboo shoots and mushrooms. Add stock, salt, sugar, M.S.G., and soy sauce. Stir fry, and if necessary add cornflour mixed with a little water to thicken sauce. Serve noodles on plate or bowl and cover with ingredients. Alternatively mix together and serve.

Chinese Chicken Curry

1 chicken breast
2 oz. curry sauce concentrate
300 ml chicken stock
2 oz roughly chopped onion
1 tsp. MSG
Sesame or vegetable oil for frying

Chop the chicken up into small ½ inch dice. Heat the wok with the oil until it is slightly smoking. Add the chicken to the wok and keep moving around for about 1 minute.

Add the onions. Again keep the ingredients on the move.

Keep the chicken and onions cooking for a further minute and then add the concentrate and once this is in the wok add the chicken stock. Stir the mixture until the concentrate is fully mixed in with the stock.

After about a minute the sauce will start to thicken up. If the sauce gets too thick, add some more stock or if too thin, add some more concentrate.

Once the sauce is about the right consistency, add the MSG stir and serve.

Chicken Chop Suey

4oz. Chicken (Breast)
1oz. Water Chestnuts
1oz. Bamboo Shoots
1oz. Mushrooms (Button)
1oz. Carrot (Matchstick size)
2oz. Beanshoots
1 Small Onion
2 Tbsp. Veg. Oil
Salt to taste
1/2 tsp. Sugar
1/2 tsp. M.S.G.
2 tsp. Soy Sauce
3 fl/oz. Chicken Stock. (or cube)
Cornflour

Thinly slice chicken. Thinly slice onion and bamboo shoots. Cut water chestnuts into three pieces and mushrooms into halves or quarters depending on size. Cut carrot into matchstick size. Wash and drain bean shoots. Heat oil in wok, add onion and stir fry. Add chicken. Add carrot and water chestnuts. Stir fry adding mushrooms and bamboo shoots. Add bean shoots and stir fry adding stock, salt, sugar, M.S.G., and soy sauce. If necessary add cornflour mixed with a little water to thicken sauce. Serve on plate or bowl.

Sweet and sour chicken

4oz. Chicken (Pre-Cooked).
2 oz onion
1 oz carrot
4oz. Self Raising Flour.
Veg. Oil (For Deep Frying).

Sweet and Sour Sauce. (See Sauces).

Cut chicken (Pre-Cooked) into cubes about one inch square. Make Sweet and sour sauce(See Sauces). Make batter by adding self raising flour with cold water. Whisk into a stiff batter, but one which flows freely. Heat oil in wok for deep frying. Dip each piece of pork into batter. Deep fry until! crisp and golden brown. Alternatively dip each piece of pork into egg white and slave through corn flour. Deep fry. Use plate or bowl to serve with rice or chips and sweet and sour sauce.

Chicken in Yellow bean Sauce with cashews

4 oz Chicken
1 fresh green chilli
1 tbsp yellow bean paste
1tbsp Hoi Sin sauce
Cornflour
Sesame Oik
2 oz cashew nuts

Cut the chicken into thin, even strips. De-seed and slice the chilli into fine rings.
Combine the yellow bean paste, and Hoi Sin sauce together in a bowl. Then mix the cornflour with water until smooth, then add to the paste mixture.
Heat half the oil in a wok low heat and brown cashews evenly. Remove from pan.
Add the remaining oil to the pan and increase to a high heat. Add the chicken and chilli and stir-fry for 2 - 3 minutes until sealed on all sides.
Add the sauce to the pan and stir over a medium heat until the chicken is evenly glazed and the sauce is thickened.
Add the cashew nuts and serve at once.

Lemon Chicken

1lb (450g) chicken cut into strips
salt and pepper to taste
1 tbsp chinese rice wine
1 egg lightly beaten
2 tbsp plain flour blended with 1 tbsp of water
oil for deep frying
7 floz (200ml) ready made lemon sauce (see lemon sauce recipe)
slices of fresh lemon to garnish

Trim the chicken meat. Marinate in the salt, pepper and wine for 25-30 minutes. coat the chickcen with the egg and flour paste. Deep fry the chicken pieces in hot oil (180/350) until golden brown. Remove and drain. cut each breast into bite size pieces and arrange on a serving dish. Heat 1 tbsp of oil in a wok or saucepan and mix in the lemon sauce (see separate recipe) blend well and pour evenly over the chicken. garnish with the lemon slices and serve hot.

Chicken with bamboo shoots and water chestnuts

4oz. Chicken (Breast).
2oz. Water Chestnuts.
1oz. Bamboo Shoots.
1 Small Onion.
2 Tbsp. Veg. Oil.
Salt to Taste.
1/2 tsp. Sugar.
1/2 tsp. M.S.G.
2 tsp. Soy Sauce.
3 fl/oz. Chicken Stock (or cube).
Cornflour.

Thinly slice chicken. Thinly slice onion and bamboo shoots. Cut water chestnuts into three pieces. Heat oil in wok. Add onion and stir fry, adding chicken. Continue stir fry and add water chestnuts and bamboo shoots. Add salt, sugar, M.S.G., and soy sauce. Stir fry. Serve on plate or bowl with rice or chips.

Chicken with pineapple

4oz. Chicken (Breast)
3oz. Pineapple Rings (Tinned)
1 Small Onion
2 Tbsp. Pineapple Juice
2 Tbsp. Veg. Oil
Salt to taste
1/2 tsp. Sugar
1/2 tsp. M.S.G.
2 tsp. Soy Sauce
3 fl/oz. Chicken Stock (or cube)
Cornflour

Thinly slice chicken. Thinly slice onion. Cut pineapple rings into four or five pieces. Heat oil in wok. Add onion and stir fry, adding chicken. Continue stir and add pineapple. Add stock, salt, sugar, M.S.G., and soy sauce. Stir fry adding pineapple juice. Add cornflour mixed with water to thicken sauce. Serve on plate or bowl with rice or chips.

Pork Dishes

Chinese Roast Pork

4 Tbsp. Soy sauce
4 Tbsp. Sugar
1/2 tsp. Salt
3 Tbsp. Yellow bean sauce
2 Tbsp. Hoi sin sauce
2 Garlic moons (mashed)
3 inches fresh ginger, peeled and sliced Ginger
1/2 tsp Five Spice Power
4 Star anise
1 Small onion
Dash of red powder (for colouring)

11/2 lbs lean pork.
4 Tbsp. Golden syrup.

Cut pork into strips about 4inches by 2 inches Mix all marinade ingredients in large bowl. Add pork strips and mix in well. Marinate for several hours. Place pork strips on roasting tray and cook in hot oven for about fifteen minutes. Turn and cook for a further ten minutes. Remove from oven and brush on golden syrup, which has been melted down. Roast until ribs are a golden reddish brown. They can be stored in fridge or freezer for future use.

Crispy Pork Balls

1 Pork tenderloin cooked
1 teaspoon salt
6 tbsp thick cornflour paste
1 pint seasoned oil
1 tbsp Chinese rice wine
1 teaspoon MSG
4 Slices stale bread
1 tbsp sesame oil
1 Cup plain flour
200ml water
20ml water

Chop cooked pork into 1cm cubes. Remove the crusts from the bread and break into small pieces in a bowl and add a little water to make a thick dough. Roll a ball of the bread dough around each piece of pork. Make a thick batter with 1 cup of the flour, seasoned with the salt and MSG and the 200ml water. Mix gently with a fork. Heat the seasoned oil and sesame oil in a hot wok to 190 degrees. Dip each ball in the batter and deep fry in small batches until golden brown. Stir regularly to prevent sticking. Serve with sweet and sour sauce.

Sweet and Sour Pork

4oz. Pork (Pre-Cooked)
1 Small Onion
1 Small Carrot
4oz. Self raising Flour
Veg. Oil (For Deep Frying)
Sweet and Sour Sauce. (See Sauces)
Egg White
Cornflour

Cut Pork (Pre-Cooked) into cubes about one inch square. Make Sweet and sour sauce(See Sauces). Make batter by adding self raising flour with cold water. Whisk into a stiff batter, but one which flows freely. Heat oil in wok for deep frying. Dip each piece of pork into batter. Deep fry until! crisp and golden brown. Alternatively dip each piece of pork into egg white and slave through corn flour. Deep fry. Use plate or bowl to serve with rice or chips and sweet and sour sauce.

Hot, sweet and Spicy Chinese Roast Pork with beansprouts

4oz. Chinese Roast Pork (Pre-Cooked).
4oz. Beanshoots.
1oz. Carrot (Matchstick Size).
1 Small Onion.
1 Tbsp. Garden Peas.
1 Tbsp. Chicken Stock.
2 Tbsp. Veg. Oil.
Hot Sweet and Spicy Sauce.

Thinly slice Chinese Roast Pork. Thinly slice onion and cut carrot into matchstick size. Wash and drain beanshoots. Make Sauce(see sauces). Heat oil in wok. Add onion and stir fry, adding carrot. Add Chinese roast pork then beanshoots and peas. Add stock and quickly stir fry until stock is reduced. Add sauce and mix in well.

Chinese Roast Pork Chow Mein

4oz. Chinese Roast pork
4oz. Fine Noodles
1oz. Mushrooms (Button)
1oz. Bamboo Shoots
2oz. Beanshoots
1 Small Onion
3 Tbsp. Veg. Oil
Salt to taste
1/2 tsp. Sugar
1/2 tsp. M. S.G.
2 tsp. Soy Sauce
3 fl/oz. Chicken Stock
Cornflour

Put noodles in half pot of boiling water. Stir to loosen strands and drain. Thinly slice onion, Chinese roast pork, and bamboo shoots. Cut mushrooms across into four or five pieces. Wash and drain beanshoots. Heat 1 Tbsp. of oil in wok. Add noodles and stir fry, tossing to prevent sticking. Add beanshoots and stir fry. Put at one side. Heat 2 Tbsp. of oil in wok, add onion and stir fry adding bamboo shoots and mushrooms. Stir fry and add Chinese roast pork, stock, salt, sugar, M.S.G., and soy sauce. Stir fry, and if necessary add cornflour mixed with a little water to thicken sauce. Serve noodles on plate or bowl and cover with ingredients. Alternatively mix together and serve.

Pork with Tomatoes

4oz. Lean Pork
3oz. Tomatoes (fresh)
1 Small Onion
2 Tbsp. Veg. Oil
Salt to taste
1/2 tsp. Sugar
1/2 tsp. M.S.G.
2 tsp. Soy Sauce
3 fl/oz. Chicken Stock (or cube)
Cornflour

Thinly slice pork. Thinly slice onion. Cut tomatoes into halves or quarters if larger size. Heat oil in wok. Add onion and stir fry, adding pork. Continue stir fry and add tomatoes. Add stock, salt, sugar, M.S.G., and soy sauce. Stir fry or toss, keeping tomato quarters as whole as possible. If necessary add cornflour mixed with water to thicken sauce. Serve on plate or bowl with rice or chips.

Pork with mushrooms

4oz. Lean Pork
3oz. Mushrooms
1 Small Onion
2 Tbsp. Veg. Oil
Salt to taste
1/2 tsp. Sugar
1/2 tsp. M.S.G.
2 tsp. Soy Sauce
3 fl/oz. Chicken Stock
Cornflour

Thinly slice pork. Thinly slice onion. Cut mushrooms into halves or quarters if larger size. Heat oil in wok. Add onion and stir fry, Adding chicken. Continue stir fry and add mushrooms. Add stock, salt, sugar, M.S.G., and soy sauce. Stir fry and if necessary add cornflour mixed with water to thicken sauce. Serve on plate or bowl with rice or chips.

Pork with bamboo shoots and water chestnuts

4oz. Lean Pork
2oz. Water Chestnuts
1oz. Bamboo shoots
1 Small Onion
2 Tbsp. Veg. Oil
Salt to taste
1/2 tsp. Sugar
1/2 tsp M.S.G.
2 tsp. Soy Sauce
3 fl/oz. Chicken Stock
Cornflour

Thinly slice pork. Thinly slice onion and bamboo shoots. Cut water chestnuts into three pieces. Heat oil in wok. Add onion and stir fry, adding pork. Continue stir fry and add water chestnuts and bamboo shoots. Add stock, salt, sugar, M.S.G., and soy sauce. Stir fry and if necessary add cornflour mixed with water to thicken sauce. Serve on plate or bowl with rice or chips.

Pork with green peppers and black bean sauce

4oz. Lean Pork
3oz. Green Peppers
1 Small Onion
2 tsp. Veg. Oil
Salt to taste
1/2 tsp. Sugar
1/2 tsp. M.S.G
2 tsp. Soy Sauce.
3 tbsp. Black Bean Sauce.
3 fl/oz. Chicken Stock.
Cornflour.

Thinly Slice pork. Thinly slice onion. Cut green peppers into squares. Heat oil in wok. Add onion and stir fry, adding pork. Continue stir fry and add peppers. Add stock, Salt, sugar, M.S.G., and soy sauce. Stir fry and add blackbean sauce. Mix in well. if necessary add cornflour mixed with water to thicken sauce. Serve on plate bowl with rice or chips.

Special Dishes

Special Foo Yung
1oz. King Prawn
1oz. Chicken (Breast)
1oz. Chinese Roast Pork (Pre-cooked)
3 Eggs
1 Small Onion
1 Tbsp. Veg. Oil
Salt to taste
1/2 tsp. Sugar
1/2 tsp. M. S.G.
1 tsp. Soy Sauce
Dash of Yellow Powder (For Colour)

Shell King Prawns and slice down back to remove veins. Thoroughly rinse. Thinly slice chicken, Chinese roast pork and onion. Beat eggs in bowl and add a dash of yellow powder for colouring. Heat oil in wok. Add onion and stir fry, adding chicken. Add prawns, Chinese roast pork and peas. Stir fry adding salt, sugar, M.S.G and soy sauce. Make well in centre and add eggs. Gently turn into centre with slicer or toss contents and cook for about one minute more. Serve on plate or bowl with rice or chips.

It is easier to use frozen prawns that have already been shelled and deveined. Try to buy Frozen but raw prawns and defrost properly before use.

Special Omelette

1oz. King Prawns
1oz. Chicken (Breast)
1oz. Chinese Roast Pork. (Pre-Cooked)
1oz. Mushrooms (Button)
3 Eggs
1 Small Onion
1 Tbsp. Garden Peas
2 Tbsp. Veg. Oil
Salt to taste
1/2 tsp. Sugar
1/2 tsp. M.S.G.
1 tsp. Soy Sauce
1 Tbsp. Chicken Stock (or cube)
Dash of yellow powder (for colour)

Shell prawns and slice down back to remove veins. Thoroughly rinse. Thinly slice chicken and Chinese roast pork. Thinly slice onion and cut mushrooms into four or five pieces. Beat eggs in bowl, adding a dash of yellow powder for colour. Heat 2 Tbsp. of oil in wok. Add onion and Stir fry, adding chicken. Continue stir fry and add mushrooms and peas. Add prawns and Chinese roast pork. Stir fry and add stock. salt, sugar, M.S.G., and soy sauce. Stir fry and put at one side.

Heat the remainder of the oil in the wok. Pour in egg mixture and use a circular motion to form omelette. Place cooked ingredients on omelette part nearest to you. Using a slicer, fold over and fold in sides until ingredients are fully enclosed. Serve on plate with rice or chips.

Singapore Fried Rice

peanut oil
One egg (cracked)
1 clove of garlic finely chopped
1 green chilli very finely chopped
Two cups of pre cooked (steamed) jasmine rice (left in fridge overnight)
A 1/4 each of yellow, green and red pepper "julienned"
A generous pinch of salt, sugar and msg
6 cooked king prawns (each cut into 3) pre cooked chicken can also used
1/4 cup of petit pois
1 level tsp of chilli powder (more if you like the heat)
1 tsp curry sauce
1 tsp of light soy sauce
2 spring onions chopped diagonally for garnish

Heat the oil in a wok
Add the egg and stir fry 30 seconds appx
Add garlic and chilli all the time stir frying
Add the rice keep stir frying
Add the 3 julienned peppers
Add salt, sugar and MSG
Add the prawns
Add the peas
Add the chilli powder
Add the curry sauce
Add the soy sauce
Add the spring onions

Acknowledgements

Many thanks to all of the people who helped immensely in providing and testing all of these recipes. You are all very, very special people!

Michelle and Clive W, for the testing, Rachel C for useful comments on proof reading and of course Big Tony J for showing me the correct use of a hok. (Please, next time Tony, can you show me on food though!)

Printed in Great Britain
by Amazon.co.uk, Ltd.,
Marston Gate.